CREATIVE WORSHIP
Lynn M. Hayden

Creative Worship
Lynn M. Hayden

MOVEMENT IDEAS FOR PRAISE AND WORSHIP

"But the hour is coming, and now is, when the true worshipers will worship the Father in spirit and truth; for the Father is seeking such to worship Him."

John 4:23

Second Edition 2006

© 2002, Lynn M. Hayden

Dancing For Him Ministries, Inc.

ISBN: 0-9771925-5-5

All rights are reserved. This book is protected under the copyright laws of the United States of America. This reference guide may not be reprinted or copied for commercial gain or profit. The use of short quotations or occasional page copying for personal or group study is permitted and encouraged. No permission is necessary for that.

Book Design: Jessica Mitchem

Book Production: SPS Publications, Eustis, FL

spsbooks.com

Table of Contents

Introduction 7

Mirrors & Echoes 9

Planned Spontaneity 17

Group Shapes 25

North, South, East, West 35

Body Sculpting 41

Unison Movement 47

Monologues 53

Background—Foreground 57

Conclusion 63

Introduction

As it is written on the back cover, the purpose of these Creative Worship exercises is:

- To stimulate and activate spontaneity
- To activate leadership skills
- To stimulate creativity during team ministry
- To cultivate unity and harmony among team members
- To expand movement ideas for praise and worship

This booklet was born out of years of observation and participation in worship dance locally, and around the world. In my travels, I noticed many dance teams that worshipped beautifully, but often needed help with continuity, unity, and flow. There are many times during a worship service, where each dancer dances individually, with the team. In other words, everyone is dancing all at the same time, but doing their own movements. This book will show many ideas about dancing together in various shapes and unified formations.

Over the years, during many worship dance workshops, the Lord has helped me develop several exercises to help teams worship more closely, with unified creativity and flow. This is not to say that praise and worship should be planned or choreographed (although for some that would prove to be a little easier). This is to give those who spontaneously dance (either often or on occasion), some creative ideas so their worship may minister effectively. I encourage you to use these exercises during your dance team practice times or during your own workshops. So when it comes time to dance spontaneously, during worship, you and your team will have a well of fresh ideas from which to draw.

CHAPTER 1
MIRRORS & ECHOS

Purpose

Mirror—To activate the dancer in following another, so that during spontaneous dancing, it appears as though it is choreographed. This has a wonderful effect and is often impressive, particularly if several people are involved.

Echo—Although these exercises are much more difficult and require some practice, they can have a nice element of surprise that adds variety and interest to both spontaneous as well as choreographed dances.

Exercises

MIRROR Pairs: Everyone get with a partner and begin by facing each other. Get fairly close, as if you were looking into a mirror. Someone take the initiative and be the leader, while the other one follows exactly. After a while, the other person becomes the leader. The movements will need to be pretty much two dimensional. This is good practice for the other exercises.

Once each person has had a turn, then repeat the same exercise only have one person behind the other. At this point, you may do movements that are a little more three dimensional. Switch leaders for a while.

Then do the same exercise, taking turns, with

one person on their knees (or lunging if it is too hard on the knees), and the person behind, still following exactly only with upper body movements. The variation in levels adds interest, depth, and dimension.

MIRROR Groups: Once everyone gets the hang of this, it is nice to get in groups of four to six people on varying levels. For example: have one kneeling (by sitting on their feet); one kneeling up; one in a low lunge; one in a near-standing lunge; and one person in the back standing straight. Everyone follows the arm and upper body movements of the person that is kneeling all the way in the front. This is very anointed and visually stimulating.

During a worship service, it is a good idea to not switch people around. However, during your practice times or a workshop, it is wonderful to see the variety that is created when you rotate people (so that every one gets a turn in a different position). It is also nice to take turns sitting out to watch. This way, everyone gets the idea and is able to see how powerful it is.

ECHO Pairs: Stop/Start - Take turns being the

leader and face each other. The leader should do a very simple movement to four slow counts, then hold the pose for four more counts.

The follower would do what the leader did on the first four counts only start on the second four counts. It would go something like this:

Leader—move on 1,2,3,4, hold on 5,6,7,8

Follower—hold on 1,2,3,4, begin doing what the leader did on 5,6,7,8

Leader—different move on 1,2,3,4, hold on 5,6,7,8

Follower—hold the previous pose for 1,2,3,4 do new copied move on 5,6,7,8

One behind the other: Do the same exercise as above, only take turns one behind the other and facing front.

Once you get used to working with one another, then you may be more ready to try continuous movement (not pausing or holding). This takes quite a bit of practice and the leader must keep the movements simple enough for the follower to remember and execute.

MIRROR & ECHO Groups: This exercise can be developed into movement ideas that may be incorporated into your choreographed dances.

Again, this is visually stimulating and adds variety to spontaneous (as well as choreographed) dances.

Divide the group in half, and have them face each other. One person lead one side and another one lead the other. All the members of each group should follow their respective leaders. One group's leader should begin the movements, while the other group's leader follows (or mirrors) him or her.

A greater challenge would be for one leader to start with simple movements and hold the pose for four counts (just like we did with pairs), while the second group's leader echoes that movement. Of course, each group follows only their respective leader.

A step further, yet similar would be to do a question and answer type of movement. One leader would start with a movement, then the second leader would echo with a corresponding or even opposing movement.

This looks really great when one group does a high-reach-to-the-sky move, and the other group does a low sweeping movement, and then alternate.

That was all just practice. Now, the really fun and very interesting exercise is to combine both groups. First, stagger and scatter groups one and two, so that everyone is kind of evenly distributed. Then, do the same exercise with the same leaders. Again, each group follows their own leader for a very dramatic effect. Try it with different types of music. You'll love the outcome!

CHAPTER 2

PLANNED SPONTANIETY

Purpose

To teach the worship dancer how to quickly interpret, plan, and organize a dance team for praise or worship, with very little song list notice.

Some dance teams have the luxury of acquiring the Sunday or mid-week worship songs well in advance. This gives the team time to pray, think, and practice what they will be doing during those services.

Realistically, however, most teams do not know what the song list will be until about an hour before the service. To remedy this situation, there is a solution called "planned spontaneity." This seems like a contradiction in terms. However, it is exactly what it says. Part of the song is planned, and part of the song is done spontaneously.

For example: If you know that one of the songs is going to be a "river" type song, then right away, you may know to work with blue props. So let's say that if there are 5 people on the team, you may have one on either end of a blue billow cloth, two using blue flags, and one dancing. That probably took about fifteen seconds to explain. Therefore, it would only take that long to decide and direct before service. So, the people and prop placement are the "planned" parts, while the movements of all three parts (cloth, flags, and dancer), would contain the "spontaneity."

If you have something more choreographed, that will have been practiced during your team practice time, it may then only be a matter of quick staging, before worship.

Exercises

These are really examples. This type of activity could be practiced during your team practice time. For example: If you had a song like "Let the River Flow," there are several parts:

The poor man who became rich;

The lost man who became found;

The blind man who could see again;

And the dead man who was born again;

Of course, you have the chorus: Let the River Flow…

To put it all together, all you would have to do is assign parts so each one could dramatically act out theirs, and have a leader lead everyone in the chorus. You could make it as simple or complicated as time will allow.

Here is another example, with a two fold purpose. If you have a song that is long and repetitive, the best thing to do is change around your group's positioning on the floor and/or stage.

Let's say the whole team would start in a tight knight group on the floor (in between the seats and the alter area), with their backs to the congregation. Simple step one would be to all follow the leader's movements, who is in the front of the group (overhead movements look best and may be best accomplished due to spatial constraints).

Step two would be (after a little while in the song), for the group to follow the leader up a couple of steps, toward the plat-  form (if it is conducive). Everyone still follows the leader for a while. Then the next step would be for the whole group to follow the leader onto the platform.

Once up on the platform, the leader indicates that it is time to turn around. At that point, the person who was last in the group, now becomes the leader.

After following that leader for a while, one designated person, on the side of the group, could step out of the group, go to the other side of the stage and do a spontaneous solo, while the rest of the group continues to follow leader two.

A side note here is that when the side person "breaks out," they should try to use the same arm movements as the group during the transition away. Also, as they then return to the group, they should try to pick up what ever arm movements are being done at the time of transition.

If the song is still going on, a second side person may step out and do a solo, using transition movements to get to the side of the stage.

Finally, if the song still continues to be long and repetitive, you could make a group formation, (similar to what was done in the mirrors section). This is where leader number two goes on the knees, while everyone else poses in varying levels, and still follows the leader's arm movements.

The somewhat tricky part here is that people have a tendency to really follow the leader.

If it is not mentioned ahead of time, everyone will naturally just kneel (which is not very effective). It is best to mention well in advance that when you get to the place on the stage where the leader kneels, that everyone knows to "clump" (or get in a varied position group setting).

Finally, all may rise and exit as the song comes to an end. The variations are endless, but this gives you  some ideas of what to do during a long song, so that it is not monotonous to watch or do. Also, most of this dance is spontaneous, where as the "planned" directions would only take seconds to decide and direct.

CHAPTER 3
GROUP SHAPES

Purpose

To stimulate and activate spontaneity. To activate leadership skills. To stimulate creativity during team ministry. To cultivate unity and harmony among team members. To expand movement ideas for praise and worship as well as choreography.

So often, we tend to choreograph with an even amount of space around ourselves. It is socially acceptable to have a certain amount of space between ourselves and another human being. When a person steps into our sphere of comfort ability, we tend to very quickly become uncomfortable.

This seems to carry over into our spontaneous and choreographed dancing. These exercises will help to break the mold, as it were, and get us thinking with anti-spatial depth perception.

Exercises

In a small group of about four or five, get close together and create a shape. Strike a pose. It is as if the group as a whole becomes an abstract sculpture. Arms and legs should be everywhere and intertwined. No one knows how an other person is going to pose.

Quick Change

Try it with music where you quickly strike a pose on count one, and hold it for the remaining three counts. It would be like: Pose, 2,3,4. Then change the pose and hold again. Evolve in to a pose, hold another time and keep doing this for around sixteen to thirty-two counts, until everyone feels comfortable.

Slow Change

Also, this same exercise could be done to eight counts only instead of striking a pose, quickly, and holding, you could move through the music to arrive at a pose by count seven.

It could be something like: Move, 2,3,4,5,6, pose, hold. Then move, 2,3,4,5,6, pose, hold.

Weight Bearing

This is another nice effect that could be practiced with or with out music. Actually, it would probably be better to get into the positions slowly without music, until you are used to getting there.

Have some of the shapes be weight bearing. This would be where two or more people in the group either pull on one another, push on one another or rest upon someone.

For example: Two of the people in the group could stand as if they are shaking hands only they would lean back by pulling on each other's hands (or wrists). They could rest upon on each other's feet for support or balance.

Then, two more people could, say, reach their arms over the other two and push each other's hands (as if they were trying to bulldoze down a wall).

Finally, if there is any one left, they could rest against someone's back. The possibilities are endless.

Reflecting

This is one of my favorites. Have each person in the group take a turn being the shape leader. Everyone strikes a pose, but it must reflect the leader's pose in some manner.

For example: if the person in the front stands  with their arms straight out in front of them and they have their legs apart, and then bend both knees, then the rest of the group must make similar shapes.

Let's say one person on a side would have similar arm placement, only their back arm would be higher then the front. Instead of facing directly front, they could angle out to the side, slightly, and instead of having the legs apart, with knees bent, they could have legs together and bent.

The other person on the other side, could have a similar pose as the front person, only have a bend in the elbows, like they are resting their arms on a huge chair's arms. Then, perhaps, in this pose, they could lift one leg and lean side ways (away from the center of the group).

Finally, perhaps a person standing in the back could stand straight up and have both arms reach high, over head.

This type of activity creates very interesting designs. After all, dance is art and art is about design and our God is a creative designer who loves creativity!

Stage Space Change

As a group, congregate all together, first, only this time, have two leaders with in the group. Have one of them be the main leader.

Start out by all following the timing and possibly the design of leader one. Then at some point, have the second leader take a couple of the people over to the side of the stage or to another area. They would create their own shapes and poses to the music, while the main leader remains in the center (or another area) with the other half of the group, doing their own rendition of sculptural design.

At some point, they come together again and either follow their own leader or reflect the main leader again, and all make one final pose.

This kind of exercise can very easily be done as interpretive, spontaneous dancing, as well. In other words, instead of holding poses, the respective groups could follow their leaders in interpretive movement as well.

One giant group shape

This is a fun exercise for a large group or conference. It is something that can activate spontaneity, creativity, and group design ideas. It could be incorporated into worship or choreography as a point of interest.

Start with people in each of the four corners of the stage space. One person run or walk to the center and make a pose. Then, the other three follow suit, one at a time. Once all four have made a pose, the number one person leaves and a number five person takes their place. Then a number six person takes the place of the number two person, and so on, until everyone has gotten a turn. Finally, one at a time, all the people go in and make a giant group shape.

If you have a group of about four to five people, this may be easily added into worship or choreography by running in, making the pose, then dispersing and going on to something else. One large group shape, also makes for a great ending to a dance.

All these shape exercises can be done for activation practice, but after a while, your group will become comfortable working with one another, and you may find certain poses, shapes, or reflective and weight bearing concepts that would be stunning for a section or ending of a dance.

CHAPTER 4

NORTH, SOUTH, EAST, WEST

Purpose

To activate team ministry for effective leading in a small space. To cultivate leadership and movement skills when facing different directions in the space. To overcome the problem of directional following, when the leader is temporarily out of the group's sight.

This is a solution to an age old problem. Many times, there is little space for the dance team between the seats and the alter area. Therefore, the dancers are often confined to one or two thin rows, with a leader out front (almost going down the center aisle). When everyone is facing front and all are following the leader, there is no problem with visibility. Everyone can see the leader.

The moment that the leader turns directly to the right, let's say, then all the people to the right can no longer see the leader. Likewise, when the leader turns to the left, the people on the right can relax their necks (from straining to see), but the people on the left, now, can no longer see. If everyone were to turn to the back (or toward the alter area) for a moment, then no one would be able to see.

To solve this problem, the North, South, East, West exercise was devised.

Exercises

Begin by getting into groups of four or five. If there are four people, have everyone face the front, and have that direction be North. Have the person in the front, be the North person. Subsequently, have one side person be East, one side person be West, and of course, the person in the back be South. If there is a fifth person, they should go in the middle of the group.

Close Knit

This first exercise, the whole group should be close together and do primarily upper body and arm movements. It can be done to slow or fast music.

Once the music begins, everyone mirror North's movements. After a while, the North person decides to face a different direction (let's say East). As that person turns to face that direction, they would indicate, through eye contact, that it is the East person's turn to lead. So, as everyone faces East, they all follow the East leader's movements.

Likewise, at a certain point, the East person turns to someone else (let's say West or South), and signals for them to lead. Everyone gets a turn, hence resolving the problem of not being able to see.

Loosely Knit

Another way this can be accomplished, is to be in the same type of formations, only be further apart from one another. Do the same type of exercise, only this time, do more full body movements and have more spatial activity. In other words, use up more of your space when you move (rather then staying in one place).

This can be very effective, when you all move together, as a group.

Doing the North, South, East, West formation is a very efficient way to worship and not worry, during spontaneous dance.

CHAPTER 5

BODY SCULPTING

Purpose

To activate the worship dancer in creative design; To learn obedience and submission to an artistic leader; To prepare for artistic, and dramatic presentations that coincide with a Pastor's message.

This exercise is truly awesome to watch. It can be used to dramatically enhance a topic or scripture in a sermon. It can also be done as an artistic prelude to a dance. It is like a picture that paints a thousand words.

Exercises

Abstract

One person is chosen to be the artist. That person is given the rest of the group (of about four to five people) with which to mold like clay. This artistic sculptor then begins to shape and design the people until they become a work of art.

There is no discussion before hand and no talking while the artist is molding. The artist can not demonstrate what to do. They can only take the body parts and mold them into the appropriate shape.

For example: they could have one person stand there and they could move their arm so it is in

a palm up, raised position. Then, they could hold their cheeks and tilt their head up. They could put another person's hand on that person's shoulder, tilt person two's head up in the same direction, and lift their arm up, with palms up. They could add more people in more shapes, until they are satisfied with their creation.

Scripture or Topic

This same exercise could be done to create an actual story, topic, or scripture. This is where it has practical application.

The artist could create a picture that is unmistakable, and could relate to the topic about which will have been spoken.

For example: If the Pastor is going to talk about faith and use the scripture about Peter walking on water, that scene could easily be portrayed. The artist could create a boat (depending on how many people

with whom they have to work). Then they could have a Jesus character (out beyond) beckoning to Peter. Then they could create Peter stepping out of the boat, while the others in the boat show facial expressions of surprise, fear, disbelief, etc.

When the message the artist creates is clear, it is an extremely powerful tool with which to enhance a sermon or dance.

CHAPTER 6

UNISON MOVEMENT

Purpose

To add a new dimension of unity to dances; To enhance movement with variety; To develop teamwork skills that create harmony in movement.

This is a very interesting type of movement that adds a little variety to both spontaneous worship dancing, as well as choreographed pieces.

Although it takes a bit of concentration, with practice, it becomes easier and quite effective.

Exercises

In Place

Get into a very close, tight knit group. It doesn't matter how many people. The idea is for the whole group to move together as if they are one body.

For example: Everyone can bend forward from their waist, then reach their hands and arms out, so their elbows are by their ears. Then rotate their whole upper body around in a large circle (while their arms are still up in the air). They could then open their arms out to the side, like crosses, and all lunge to one side, then all tilt their body sideways. There is usually one person in the group who naturally becomes the leader of the movements. The rest of the group will just feel when it is time to change or move into another position. This unison movement has a powerful effect.

In space on stage

This same concept can be done by remaining in a tight knit group, but as a group, move around in the stage space. This may take a little bit more practice, but when it is accomplished, will have an even more dynamic effect.

Again, it should appear as if the whole group is a single unit, and move in complete unison around the stage. This time, not only will all the upper body movements be synchronized, but also the movements that are done to get around the stage space as well.

For example: Let's say that the whole group would step in a lunge position towards stage left. Their arms would be in that diagonal cross, that was mentioned earlier. Then everyone could move in the direction of the lunged or bent leg, to a standing position, bringing the arms overhead. This is a very basic example just to give you a visual idea of the concept. The movements and positions are endless. Although it is not recommended to do this type of movement throughout an entire dance, it definitely ads interest to a portion. It ads strength and power for emphasis as well, both in worship and choreography.

CHAPTER 7

MONOLOGUES

Purpose

To add a touch of drama to dancing; To break the dancer out of their comfort zone; To enhance a dance or sermon; To add a new level of creativity to presentations.

This activity is extremely effective because it leaves much up to the imagination. Like reading a good book, your mind is left to wonder or imagine what the scenery, people, and situations would look and be like. Of course, when some things are left to the imagination, the story, picture, or outcome, can be enhanced and magnified beyond what could be physically accomplished through basic drama or dance.

Exercises

One person gets up in front of everyone else and speaks and does poses to enact a portion of scripture. Only the key words or phrases are spoken. The rest is left up to the audience to fill in the blanks. The words must be spoken loudly, clearly, slowly, and dramatically. If a common bible story is used, that the majority of people know, it is much easier for everyone to understand.

For example: If someone were to choose the story of when Peter denies Jesus three times, they may only say a few key words that may go something like this:

Three times?!
No never!!!
You were with Him.
Not I.
Crow…
Strange.
I saw you there!
I wasn't
Crow…
Deny.
Crow…
Shame
Sorrow
Weeping…

Though it takes a little practice, the powerful, dramatic effect is worth the time and effort.

CHAPTER 8
BACKGROUND FOREGROUND

Purpose

To stimulate thinking for acquisition of new ideas for creative worship as well as choreographed dances; To incorporate unity of movement (with a small group) in the background while an individual soloist can express a variety of movements in the foreground.

This is one of my favorite exercises, as it truly ads creativity, variety and interest to dances, and can be executed in a number of ways.

Exercises

Basically, there is a person who is in the foreground or toward the front of the stage space. That person does individual movement unassociated with the remaining group in the background.

The group in the background lines up, side by side, and does all the same movements, all at the same time. One of the people in the background is the designated leader of the background group. Their movements must be simple, repetitive and unobvious. The following are different types of patterns or tempos that may be accomplished. For all exercises, use four, slow counts of eight.

The solo person does a pose and holds it for four counts, while the group does slow, continuous movements.

- The solo person does slow, continuous movement, while the group does medium tempo repetitious movement.
- The solo person does more upbeat tempo movements, while the background does poses and holds for four counts.
- The solo person does more dramatic type movement, while the group moves directionally with their feet.
- The solo person goes all out, while the group does combined movements or changes every eight counts.
- The solo person interprets to the music while the background moves in very slow motion.
- The solo person does their own movements while the background group has two leaders whose groups echo one another. Have background do two different type of movements (preferably with different levels).

Challenge: Put two groups together. One group becomes the foreground (with a leader that they can follow), and one group becomes the background also with a leader. Repeat all of the above exercises with a foreground group (instead of a solo person, and watch the creativity come alive!

Conclusion

My hope and desire is that you get many, many creative ideas through these exercises. May you work together with your dance or drama team to create harmony and unity, as well as become more cohesive as a group for dramatic presentations. Over time, there will be an ease of movement and group amalgamation.

Also, if you are a more experienced person, and have a desire to hold workshops, these exercises really work well to activate people to a new level in the creative realm.

Finally, it is my greatest hope that you find fulfillment in your worship unto our King, and that your presentations unto Him may be more anointed, and exciting, thereby minister most effectively. The ultimate goal of *creative worship* (whether done during praise and worship or in choreography) should be ministry: by creatively expressing the heart of the Father, then presenting it to and changing the hearts of the people. May your worship dance be eternally creative!

CONTACT INFORMATION

Dancing For Him Ministries, Inc.

For further information about workshops, speaking engagements, videos, and ordering more books, please feel free to contact us at:

www.dancingforhim.com